THIS BOOK BELONGS TO

_____

STRENGTHENING YOUR PRACTICE:
A DAILY PRACTICE LOG

Keeping a Meditation Journal can seem a bit daunting to some of us. However, keeping a daily sitting log is a way to strengthen your practice and see its cycles more clearly.

Keep this notebook at the place where you sit. Write down what the meditation practice is and how long it is. Then write in just one sentence the general qualities of the practice such as 'sleepy' or 'restless and disturbed' or 'calm and light' or 'filled with plans' or 'easily centered on the breath' or whatever you noticed. Then in another sentence or two, note the general qualities of your day such as 'happy', 'relaxed and spacious' or 'overworked and tense' or 'frustrated and anxious'.

At the end of the week, use the full page of notes space to review your daily notes and be aware of cycles in your daily practice and they may reflect and connect to your daily life. Particularly become aware of areas where you may be stuck and those which call for greater mindfulness and acceptance. Write down the trends that you are seeing. Write goals for yourself, or words of encouragement.

At the end of the month, consider using this space to do the same, but looking back at your entire month and the trends, etc, you notice.

Day/Date	Meditation Practice	Comments

Notes/Trends/Goals/Words of Encouragement:

Day/Date	Meditation Practice	Comments

Notes/Trends/Goals/Words of Encouragement:

Day/Date	Meditation Practice	Comments

Notes/Trends/Goals/Words of Encouragement:

Day/Date	Meditation Practice	Comments

Notes/Trends/Goals/Words of Encouragement:

Day/Date	Meditation Practice	Comments

Notes/Trends/Goals/Words of Encouragement:

Day/Date	Meditation Practice	Comments

Notes/Trends/Goals/Words of Encouragement:

Day/Date	Meditation Practice	Comments

Notes/Trends/Goals/Words of Encouragement:

Day/Date	Meditation Practice	Comments

Notes/Trends/Goals/Words of Encouragement:

_____

_____

_____

_____

_____

_____

_____

_____

_____

_____

_____

_____

_____

_____

_____

_____

_____

_____

_____

_____

_____

_____

_____

_____

Day/Date	Meditation Practice	Comments

Notes/Trends/Goals/Words of Encouragement:

Day/Date	Meditation Practice	Comments

Notes/Trends/Goals/Words of Encouragement:

Day/Date	Meditation Practice	Comments

Notes/Trends/Goals/Words of Encouragement:

Day/Date	Meditation Practice	Comments

Notes/Trends/Goals/Words of Encouragement:

Day/Date	Meditation Practice	Comments

Notes/Trends/Goals/Words of Encouragement:

Day/Date	Meditation Practice	Comments

Notes/Trends/Goals/Words of Encouragement:

Day/Date	Meditation Practice	Comments

Notes/Trends/Goals/Words of Encouragement:

Day/Date	Meditation Practice	Comments

Notes/Trends/Goals/Words of Encouragement:

Day/Date	Meditation Practice	Comments

Notes/Trends/Goals/Words of Encouragement:

Day/Date	Meditation Practice	Comments

Notes/Trends/Goals/Words of Encouragement:

Day/Date	Meditation Practice	Comments

Notes/Trends/Goals/Words of Encouragement:

Day/Date	Meditation Practice	Comments

Notes/Trends/Goals/Words of Encouragement:

Day/Date	Meditation Practice	Comments

Notes/Trends/Goals/Words of Encouragement:

Day/Date	Meditation Practice	Comments

Notes/Trends/Goals/Words of Encouragement:

Day/Date	Meditation Practice	Comments

Notes/Trends/Goals/Words of Encouragement:

Day/Date	Meditation Practice	Comments

Notes/Trends/Goals/Words of Encouragement:

Day/Date	Meditation Practice	Comments

Notes/Trends/Goals/Words of Encouragement:

Day/Date	Meditation Practice	Comments

Notes/Trends/Goals/Words of Encouragement:

Day/Date	Meditation Practice	Comments

Notes/Trends/Goals/Words of Encouragement:

Day/Date	Meditation Practice	Comments

Notes/Trends/Goals/Words of Encouragement:

Day/Date	Meditation Practice	Comments

Notes/Trends/Goals/Words of Encouragement:

Day/Date	Meditation Practice	Comments

Notes/Trends/Goals/Words of Encouragement:

Day/Date	Meditation Practice	Comments

Notes/Trends/Goals/Words of Encouragement:

Day/Date	Meditation Practice	Comments

Notes/Trends/Goals/Words of Encouragement:

Day/Date	Meditation Practice	Comments

Notes/Trends/Goals/Words of Encouragement:

Day/Date	Meditation Practice	Comments

Notes/Trends/Goals/Words of Encouragement:

Day/Date	Meditation Practice	Comments

Notes/Trends/Goals/Words of Encouragement:

Day/Date	Meditation Practice	Comments

Notes/Trends/Goals/Words of Encouragement:

Day/Date	Meditation Practice	Comments

Notes/Trends/Goals/Words of Encouragement:

Day/Date	Meditation Practice	Comments

Notes/Trends/Goals/Words of Encouragement:

Day/Date	Meditation Practice	Comments

Notes/Trends/Goals/Words of Encouragement:

Day/Date	Meditation Practice	Comments

Notes/Trends/Goals/Words of Encouragement:

Day/Date	Meditation Practice	Comments

Notes/Trends/Goals/Words of Encouragement:

Day/Date	Meditation Practice	Comments

Notes/Trends/Goals/Words of Encouragement:

Day/Date	Meditation Practice	Comments

Notes/Trends/Goals/Words of Encouragement:

Day/Date	Meditation Practice	Comments

Notes/Trends/Goals/Words of Encouragement:

Day/Date	Meditation Practice	Comments

Notes/Trends/Goals/Words of Encouragement:

Day/Date	Meditation Practice	Comments

Notes/Trends/Goals/Words of Encouragement:

Day/Date	Meditation Practice	Comments

Notes/Trends/Goals/Words of Encouragement:

Day/Date	Meditation Practice	Comments

Notes/Trends/Goals/Words of Encouragement:

Day/Date	Meditation Practice	Comments

Notes/Trends/Goals/Words of Encouragement:

Day/Date	Meditation Practice	Comments

Notes/Trends/Goals/Words of Encouragement:

Day/Date	Meditation Practice	Comments

Notes/Trends/Goals/Words of Encouragement:

Day/Date	Meditation Practice	Comments

Notes/Trends/Goals/Words of Encouragement:

Day/Date	Meditation Practice	Comments

Notes/Trends/Goals/Words of Encouragement:

Day/Date	Meditation Practice	Comments

Notes/Trends/Goals/Words of Encouragement: